Kip and Pip's Trip

BY MARV ALINAS • ILLUSTRATED BY KATHLEEN PETELINSEK

This is **Kip**.

This is **Kip's** friend, **Pip**.

Kip and **Pip** took a **trip**.
They took a **trip** on a **ship**.

"I want to **skip** on the **ship**!" said **Kip**.
"I want to **flip** on the **ship**!"

"No! You will **slip**!" said **Pip**.
So **Kip** did not **skip**.

"We can eat a snack," said **Pip**.
Kip and **Pip** had **chips** and **dip**.

"I have **dip** on my **lip**!" said **Kip**.
"Oh **Kip**," said **Pip**.

Kip felt his **hip**.
There was a **rip**!
"Oh **Kip**," said **Pip**.

Pip fixed the **rip** with a **zip**.

"Now we can finish our **trip**," said **Kip**.

Kip and **Pip** had fun on the **ship**.
It was a great **trip**!

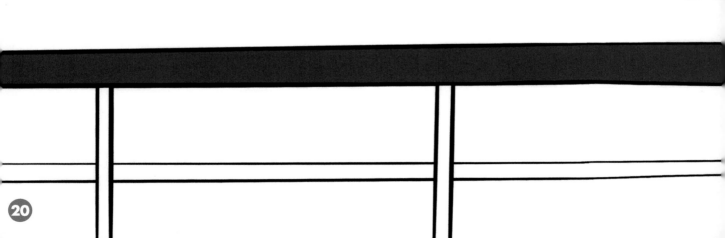

Word List

chip   rip

dip   ship

flip   skip

Kip   slip

lip   trip

Pip   zip

Which Words Rhyme?

About the Author

Marv Alinas has written dozens of books for children. When she's not reading or writing, Marv enjoys spending time with her family and traveling to interesting places. Marv lives in Minnesota.

About the Illustrator

Kathleen Petelinsek has loved to draw since she was a child. Over the years, she has designed and illustrated hundreds of books for kids. She lives in Minnesota with her husband, two dogs, and cat.

The Child's World
childsworld.com

Published by The Child's World®
1980 Lookout Drive • Mankato, MN 56003-1705
800-599-READ • www.childsworld.com

Copyright ©2019 by The Child's World®
All rights reserved. No part of this book may be reproduced or utilized in any form or by any means without written permission from the publisher.

ISBN Hardcover: 9781503827653
ISBN Paperback: 9781622434756
LCCN: 2018939259

Printed in the United States of America
PA02393